BRAVERY
ACTIVITIES FOR
MINECRAFTERS
AN UNOFFICIAL GUIDE

50 Activities to Help Kids
Build Their Courage!

ERIN FALLIGANT

Sky Pony Press
New York

Copyright © 2021 by Hollan Publishing, Inc.

Minecraft® is a registered trademark of Notch Development AB.

The Minecraft game is copyright © Mojang AB.

Sky Pony Press books may be purchased in bulk at special discounts for sales promotion, corporate gifts, fund-raising, or educational purposes. Special editions can also be created to specifications. For details, contact the Special Sales Department, Sky Pony Press, 307 West 36th Street, 11th Floor, New York, NY 10018 or info@skyhorsepublishing.com.

Sky Pony® is a registered trademark of Skyhorse Publishing, Inc.®, a Delaware corporation.

Minecraft® is a registered trademark of Notch Development AB. The Minecraft game is copyright © Mojang AB.

Visit our website at www.skyponypress.com.

10 9 8 7 6 5 4 3 2 1

Library of Congress Cataloging-in-Publication Data is available on file.

Print ISBN: 978-1-5107-6503-0

Cover design by Kai Texel
Interior design by Noora Cox
Cover illustration by Bill Greenhead
Interior illustrations by Amanda Brack

Printed in China

DEAR MINECRAFTER,

What does it mean to be brave? It means that you admit when you're scared, and you stand up to your fears when you need to. You work through your worries, and you *don't* let fear stop you from trying new things and having fun.

This book will boost your bravery with fun challenges, puzzles, and fill-in-the-blank adventures. As you explore the Overworld with your favorite characters and critters, you'll get tips and tricks that you can use in the *real* world, too. With every page, you'll grow stronger—and your fears will grow weaker.

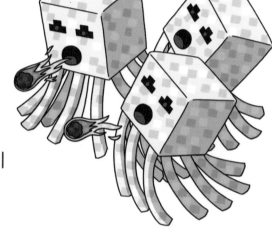

Ready to begin?

CONTENTS

WHAT IS BRAVERY?

Some people think being brave means never feeling afraid. Not true! Decode this message to learn what it *really* means.

Circle each word that comes right after the word ARMOR.

ENCHANTED ARMOR BEING YOU STRONG ARMOR BRAVE ISN'T ALWAYS ARMOR MEANS THE SAME THING AS ARMOR DOING YOUR BEST ARMOR OR ARMOR FACING ARMOR SOMETHING SOMEWHERE ARMOR EVEN IF ARMOR IF YOU ARMOR IT MIGHT MAYBE ARMOR SCARES SMILES ARMOR YOU.

Write the words you circled here:

_____

_____

WHAT FEAR FEELS LIKE

What happens to your body when you're scared?

Check off the things you've felt before:

☐ My heart pounds in my ears.

☐ My stomach feels like it's tied in knots.

☐ My knees feel as wiggly and wobbly as slime.

☐ My throat feels tight.

☐ I start to sweat, as if I were in the Nether.

☐ I breathe really fast.

☐ I just want to run away!

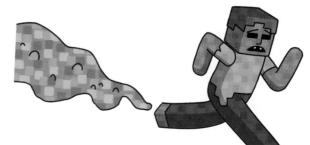

Why do you feel that way? Because your body thinks you're in danger, and it's getting you ready to fight back. If you came face to face with the Ender Dragon, you'd need to be able to fight (or get away fast!). But most times when you're scared, you're not *really* in danger. **Read on for ways to help your body calm down and keep its cool.**

FEAR ONLY GROWS

When you avoid something that scares you, your fear only grows.

"Grow" the picture below by copying it, using the grid lines as a guide. See what happens?

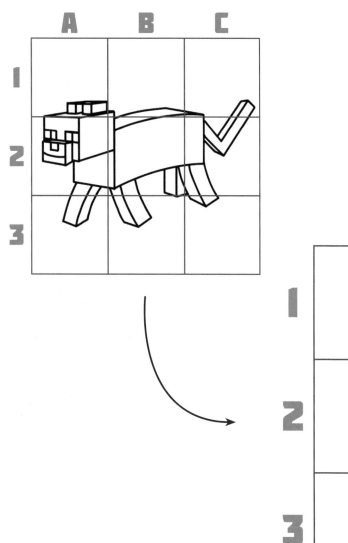

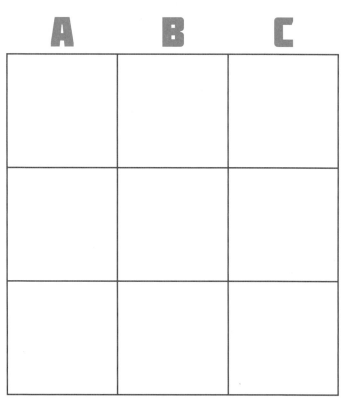

MORE REASONS TO FACE YOUR FEAR

Need more encouragement to stand up to fear?

Unscramble the words below for four more reasons.

1. Because fear is like a **E-F-H-T-I** _____.

   It can rob you of your confidence.

2. Because fear can keep you from **G-I-D-O-N** _____

   what you love and having **N-U-F** _____.

3. Because fear can **P-I-R-T** _____ you up like a tripwire and

   P-S-O-T _____ you in your tracks.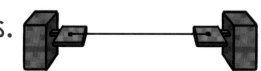

4. Because the best way to make a fear grow

   R-E-A-W-E-K _____ is to face it head-on.

IS FEAR STOPPING YOU IN YOUR TRACKS?

Take this quiz to find out.

Circle "me" next to every statement that sounds like you.

1. I won't raise my hand in class because I'm afraid of looking dumb.

   ME

   NOT ME

2. I don't try out for new sports because I'm afraid I might not be good at them.

   ME

   NOT ME

3. I say no to fun plans with friends because I'm afraid something bad might happen.

   ME

   NOT ME

4. If a friend asks me if I'm scared, I say "no way" (even if I am!).

   ME

   NOT ME

5. I stay home as much as possible because I feel safer there.

   ME

   NOT ME

IS FEAR STOPPING YOU IN YOUR TRACKS?

(continued)

6. Sometimes I can't stop thinking about the thing that scares me.

ME

NOT ME

7. I often can't fall asleep because something's freaking me out.

ME

NOT ME

8. When I see something that scares me, I sprint away like a baby villager.

ME

NOT ME

9. If I could drink a potion of Courage, I would!

ME

NOT ME

If you circled "me" 3 or more times, fear is standing in your way. There's no such thing as a potion of Courage in the real world, but there *are* ways to give your bravery a boost. **Read on!**

WORK THROUGH WORRIES

Facing fears is like mining a tunnel in Minecraft. It takes time, but if you keep trying, you'll get to a happier place.

Can you "mine" your way from worried to happy?

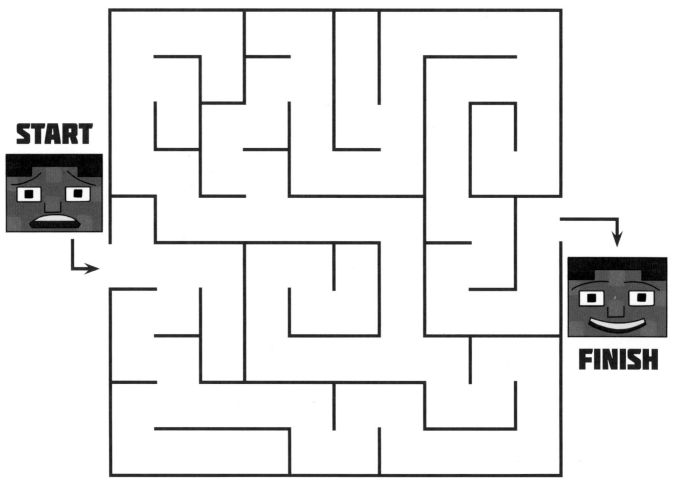

SET YOUR SIGHTS HIGH

What would you do if you had no fear? Where would you go?

Make a list of things your fear is keeping you from doing.

1. _____

2. _____

3. _____

4. _____

5. _____

This is your goal list. Sometimes it's easier to work through your worries when you *know* what you're working toward!

EVERYONE WORRIES

Everyone is scared of *something*. (If they say they're not, they're fibbing!)

Match the mobs below with the things they fear or avoid.

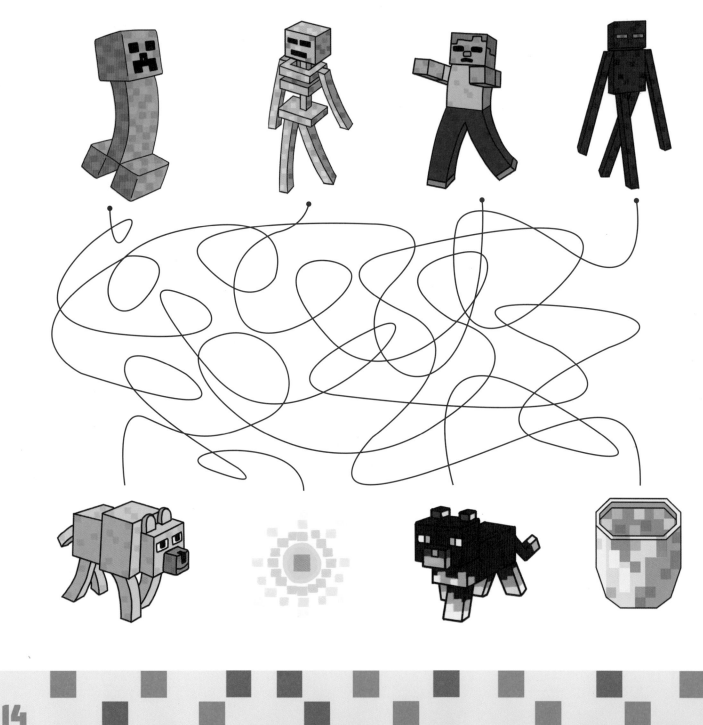

CHECK YOUR WORRIES

Here are some things that kids worry about.

Put a checkmark next to the ones that worry you.

- ☐ The dark
- ☐ Storms
- ☐ Spiders
- ☐ Being away from home
- ☐ Being left out or not making friends
- ☐ Getting sick
- ☐ Dogs

- ☐ Making mistakes
- ☐ Getting teased or bullied
- ☐ Doctor's visits
- ☐ Heights
- ☐ Grades and tests
- ☐ Getting hurt
- ☐ Talking in front of people
- ☐ Ghosts or monsters

Now cross out anything you used to be scared of, but aren't anymore. If you got past a fear, good for you! That means you can conquer *new* fears, too.

GATHER TOOLS

Think of a time when you stood up to your fear. Did you ask a friend for help? Did you tell yourself something that made you feel stronger?

Fill in what worked for you below.

I'm sometimes scared of _____,

but once I stood up to that fear. Here's what I did:

_____

_____

If I have to face a fear again, I can ask _____ for help.

I can tell myself this:

_____

_____

Reread what you wrote. These are "tools" you can use again the next time you're scared!

A BRAVE MEMORY

Picture yourself standing up to your fear.

Draw that picture below:

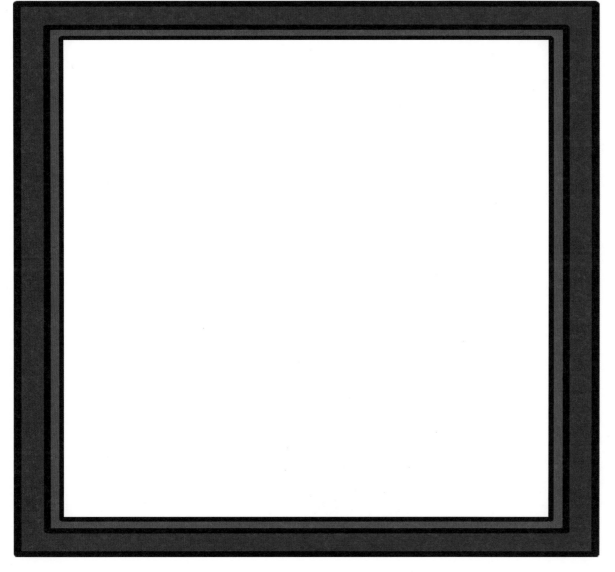

TAME YOUR FEAR

Just as you can ride a horse or pig in Minecraft, you can "tame" your fears, too. Take this quiz to find out how.

Which of these can help tame fear?

☐ Admitting my fear to someone

☐ Talking back to the thoughts in my head

☐ Dancing like crazy

☐ Coming up with mottoes that help me feel strong

☐ Giving myself a pep talk

☐ Laughing

☐ Taking a deep breath

☐ Using my imagination

☐ Eating right

☐ Getting my zzz's

ANSWERS:
ALL of these things can help tame your fear. It's true! **Read on to learn more.**

STUDY WHAT SCARES YOU

The more you know about something, the less scary it seems! Research something that's scary to you. Read a book, ask your teacher questions, or ask a parent if you can search for it online.

Share what you learn below.

What I studied: _____

Some things I learned that make it less scary: _____

_____

Something I still want to know: _____

_____

The fact is, knowing is less scary than *not* knowing. So learn as much as you can!

SHINE THE LIGHT ON FEAR

Keeping your fear a secret only makes it feel scarier. Instead of hiding it, say it out loud! Tell a friend or family member how you feel using words like the examples below.

Fill in the blanks to start your conversations.

Do you ever worry about _____ like I do?

I feel scared about _____ , but it helps me to talk about it.

Sometimes my brain goes into overdrive and I worry about _____ .

I freak out about _____ sometimes. Does that ever happen to you?

Everyone's scared of *something*. I'm scared of _____ . How about you?

BE A CHICKEN

Worried that someone will call you a chicken if you admit your fear? Let them! Chickens are *actually* pretty brave when they're defending their eggs, chicks, or turf.

Add vowels (A, E, I, and O) to the words below to reveal a clever comeback:

___ CH__CK__N?

H__Y, TH__NKS F__R

TH__ C__MPL__M__NT!

STORIES OF COURAGE

Write a story featuring YOU as a brave hero.

Use one of these prompts to get your story started:

• The mineshaft looked dark and deep. But what treasures lay below?

  [Your Name Here] _____ lit a torch and began climbing down the ladder . . .

• As a silverfish crept from the crumbling wall,

  [Your Name Here] _____ guzzled a potion of Strength and then . . .

• Would flying be more fun than scary? Time to find out. [Your Name Here] _____ tightened the Elytra wings and stepped toward the . . .

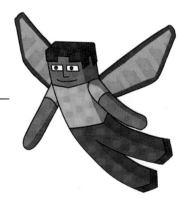

Write the rest of your story here:

_____

_____

_____

_____

_____

_____

_____

_____

Read the words out loud. How do they make you feel?

Think of a title and turn the page for your next brave step.

A COURAGEOUS COVER

Draw the book cover for your brave story below.

Add your title and the author's name—yours!

YOUR COURAGE CLUB

Who do you turn to when you need a boost of courage? Lean on those people when you need to, and be there for them when they're scared, too.

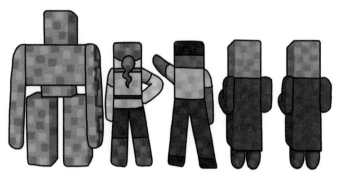

These people make me feel strong:

_____   _____

_____   _____

_____   _____

When I'm scared, they help me by _____

_____

and _____ .

If they ever feel scared, here's what I'll do: _____

_____

and _____ .

FLIP THE SWITCH

If you're thinking about something scary, "flip the switch" and turn the thought into a brave one.

Draw lines matching these scary thoughts with thoughts that will help you feel better.

1. I can't do this!

2. I'm so scared, I think I'm going to die!

3. I'm going to mess up— I know it.

4. What if everyone sees that I'm scared?

a. I might make mistakes, but that's okay. I'll do lots of things right, too.

b. I *can* do this. I've been scared before and made it through.

c. So what if they do? *Everyone* gets scared sometimes.

d. I'm not going to die. It's only fear making me feel this way, but I know how to calm myself down.

WORST CASE, BEST CASE

Are you imagining the worst-case scenario—all the bad things that could happen, even though they probably won't? Try this:

List three bad things you're worried might happen:

1. _____ ☐

2. _____ ☐

3. _____ ☐

Put a check next to any of them that you think really WILL happen. (Remember, most of them won't!)

Now list three *good* things that could happen instead:

1. _____

2. _____

3. _____

TURN "WHAT IFS" UPSIDE DOWN

Sometimes our minds play the "what if" game. *What if I make a mistake? What if everyone laughs at me?*

Write down three worries.

What if _____?

What if _____?

What if _____?

Now write the word *SO* in front of them. So what if you make a mistake? Everyone does—it's part of life. So what if people laugh? Take a bow and laugh at yourself, too! The word *so* is small but powerful. It helps you see that most worries *aren't* worth worrying about.

MEMORIZE A MOTTO

A motto is a saying that makes you feel strong.

Unscramble the words below to read each motto.

1. You're **N-T-R-O-S-G-R-E** _____

   than you think you are.

2. If you **K-N-H-T-I** _____ you can, you *will*.

3. **T-I-K-M-A-S-E-S** _____ are just

   proof that you're trying.

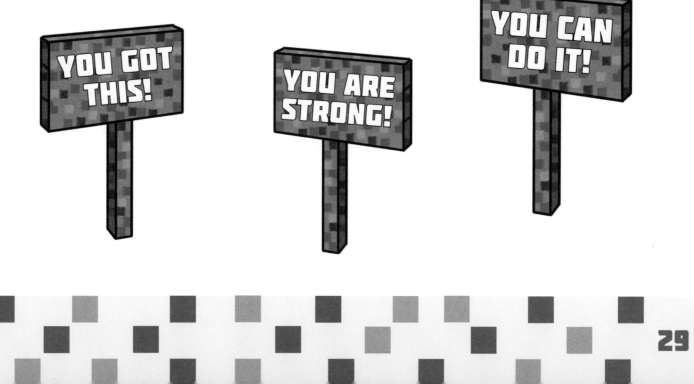

A POWERFUL STONE

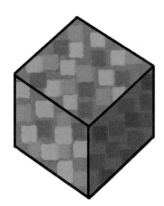

In Minecraft, messages are written on blocks of stone. You can write a message in stone, too.

Pick two or three of your favorite mottoes, and write them on the block below.

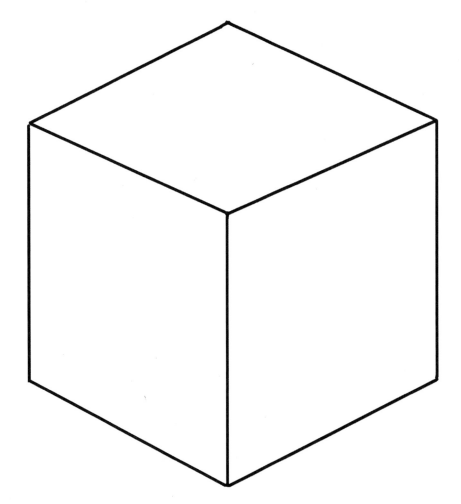

Now find a *real* stone—small enough to fit in your pocket. Paint or write a motto on the stone, and carry it with you. Touch it whenever you need a boost of bravery.

IF YOUR MIND'S STILL SPINNING

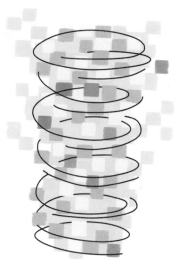

When your mind is worked up with worry, give it something *else* to think about. Which of these could work for you?

Check the ones you'd like to try.

- [ ] Read a book

- [ ] Talk to a friend

- [ ] Paint a picture

- [ ] Say the alphabet backward

- [ ] Do something kind for someone

- [ ] Memorize the lyrics to your favorite song

- [ ] Watch a funny video

GET UP AND MOVE

Another way to quiet your mind is to move your body!

Search the puzzle below, and circle every activity you can find.

WORD LIST:

BASKETBALL

DANCE

GYMNASTICS

HIKE

PUSHUPS

SITUPS

SOCCER

STRETCH

WALK

YOGA

H B Z B S P S T R E T C H D P
V I H G C V Z G F E F E S C R
F D P N Y A F H H N I N S I K
H X U H D M G H K B P M I U H
G R D C E Y N B E J U W T O G
I V A P C O W A L M J K U R A
A W A L K G Q S S J C O P M C
V X K V R A C K M T T R S E K
X Z S S O C C E R I I I O V H
T D A N C E H T H V N C N Z H
Y F I F O S J B I C G A S W H
P U S H U P S A K G N R H W F
U V S W I A X L E F V F N C B
D N L D W P Z L Z R N B Y A V
I W Y G W Z F A O L X B L N B

GET UP AND GROOVE!

Dancing is a great way to work through worries. You don't need to know any moves. Just choose tunes that make you feel strong and happy.

Create your perfect playlist. Write the names of six songs below.

1. _____

2. _____

3. _____

4. _____

5. _____

6. _____

BREATHE LIKE A PUFFERFISH

Taking deep breaths can help you feel stronger. Put your hand on your stomach. Count to 3 as you slowly inhale, feeling your belly fill up like a pufferfish. Hold your breath for a second, and then exhale, counting slowly to 4 or 5.

Take five pufferfish breaths, coloring in one fish below after taking each breath:

Hint: Coloring can take your mind off your worries, too!

FAKE IT 'TIL YOU FEEL IT

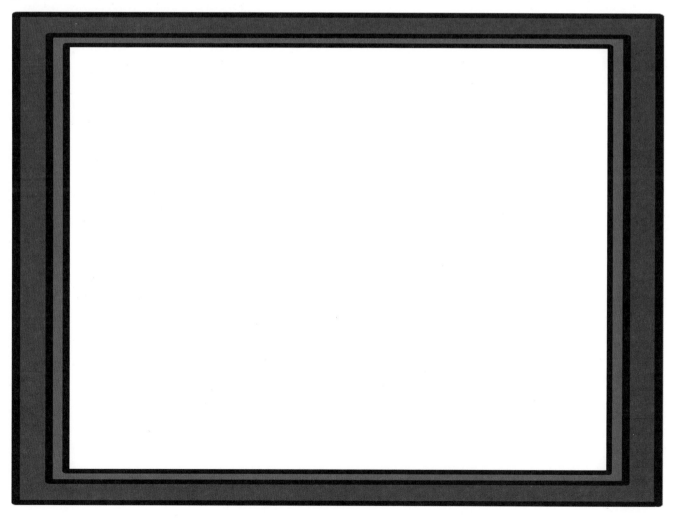

Standing in a brave pose will make you feel stronger, and the more you practice it, the braver you'll feel. Stand tall, with your shoulders back. Keep your head up and your eyes straight ahead.

Check yourself in the mirror, and then draw a picture of your brave self below.

LAUGH OUT LOUD

Feeling scared? Find something that makes you laugh—a funny video, show, or joke. You can't laugh and feel scared at the same time. It's not possible! Try this joke:

WHAT DOES AN ENDERMAN SAY WHEN IT'S BORED?

To find out, decode the message below. **Circle each word that comes right after the word ENDER.**

EMBER ENDER HEY HI THERE ENDER KID MOB CREEPER CRITTER ENDER WANT WHY HOW WHEN SHOULD ENDER TO THE NETHER AND BEYOND ENDER HAVE OR HAD AN ENDER A BRAND NEW GAME ENDER STARING AT YOU AND ME AGAIN ENDER CONTEST?

Write the words you circled here:

_____

_____

MORE POWERFUL THAN POTIONS

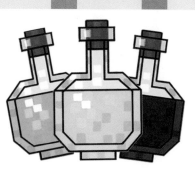

Fight fear using your powerful imagination. When you have a scary thought, imagine it floating into the air like a potion bubble. Then imagine reaching out and touching it. *Pop!* It's gone.

Write your worries on the bubbles below. Then "pop" those worries, one by one!

CATCH AND RELEASE

Another way to let go of worries is to imagine they're fish in a river. If you "catch" a worry, toss it back. If another nibbles at your line, release it from the hook and let it go. Watch it swim away, back out to sea.

Can you help this fish make its way out to sea?

FROM SCARY TO SILLY

If you start imagining something scary, tell your imagination to turn it into something silly. Practice here.

Dress up each creeper with silly accessories, like glasses, wigs, caps, and clothes.

Still scary? Not so much!

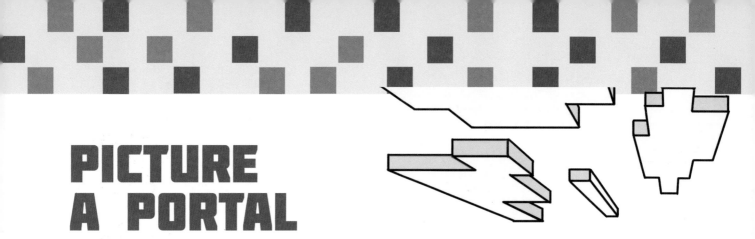

PICTURE A PORTAL

To escape your worries, take an imaginary trip to a peaceful place in the Overworld. Are you floating on a cloud? Rocking gently in a rowboat?

Fill in the blanks to write a story about your peaceful place.

I left the _____ behind and stepped through the portal.

As soon as I reached the other side, I started to relax. I could

see nothing but _____ for miles around.

I could smell _____ and hear _____.

I stretched out to enjoy the scenery, feeling the _____

beneath my _____. I gazed up at the _____,

took a deep breath, and smiled.

Read the story you wrote, and imagine it using all of your senses.

Now draw the scene in the portal below.

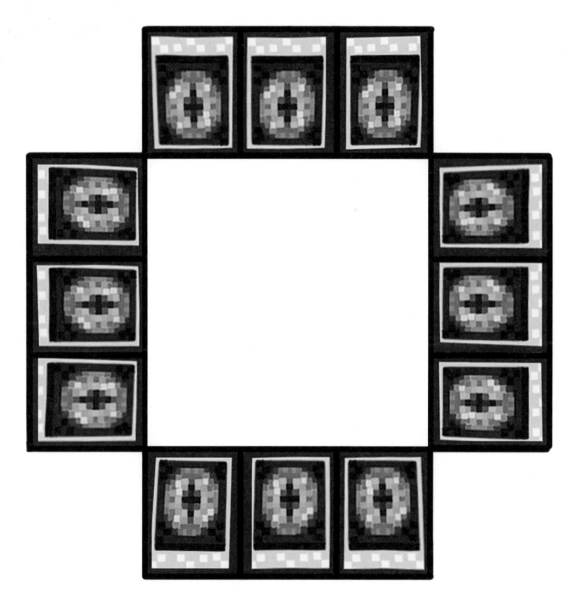

Whenever you're feeling scared, close your eyes and imagine this peaceful place. Your mind is the portal that will take you there!

SEARCH FOR HEALTHY SNACKS

When you're scared or stressed, give your body the fuel it needs to feel better.

Circle every healthy snack you can find in the puzzle below.

WORD LIST:

APPLES

BANANAS

BERRIES

CARROTS

CELERY

CHEESE

NUTS

POPCORN

RAISINS

YOGURT

```
P N H P F C O S J B R E H Z E
U R Z T Y E H C P N Y E C L U
U Y F G B Q O P N R O C A V P
N F I L Z B F N E J G A I Y X
D U Y K O Y A H X H U R Q P F
U J X Q B L D N V V R R L M C
R P A U P I C X A J T O O Y S
B D A T H O N Q B N R T B B G
P P A Z P R P L M R A S C Y E
A P P L E S I C Z D C S E R E
U P V A A E G L O N O N L L Z
H N R A I S I N S R N F E X I
V U C H E E S E V U N M R L L
W T P K M B N M V H P T Y E D
S S H D L B E R R I E S F H M
```

TUCK AWAY WORRIES

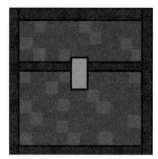

Before bed, imagine putting your worries into a treasure chest. Close the lid, lock them up, and promise yourself that you won't peek in the chest again until tomorrow.

Write your worries in the chest below.

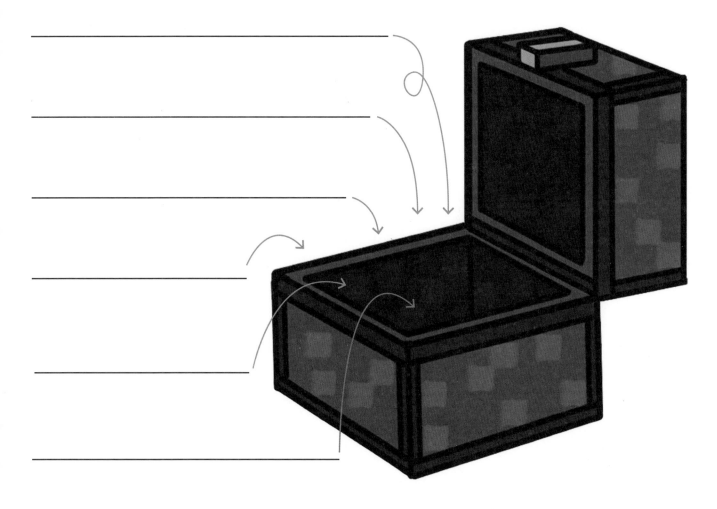

Now lock them up tight!

BE GRATEFUL

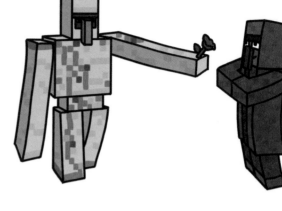

It's hard to feel scared when you're feeling thankful. Set aside time every night to think about *all* the people and things you're grateful for. Make a list. You'll fall asleep thinking happy thoughts!

Three things I'm thankful for:

1. _____

2. _____

3. _____

Three people I'm thankful for:

1. _____

2. _____

3. _____

One nice thing I can do tomorrow to say thank you:

_____

GET YOUR ZZZ'S

What are other ways to wind down so that worries won't keep you up? Create your own bedtime routine.

Would you rather...?

1. Take a warm bath   **OR**   Take a shower

2. Read a book   **OR**   Listen to music

3. Take pufferfish breaths   **OR**   Imagine your peaceful place

4. "Pop" any worries like bubbles   **OR**   Tuck them into an imaginary chest

5. Dream about flying   **OR**   Dream about building a castle in the clouds

Try to follow the same routine every night. When you do, you're telling your body and mind that it's time to unwind. And soon, they'll start to listen!

MORE STORIES OF COURAGE

Write another story featuring YOU as the brave hero.

Use one of these prompts to get your story started:

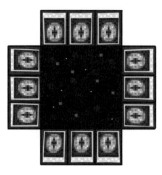

• The portal glowed. _____ knew it
[Your Name Here]

was time to enter, but what lay on the other

side? There was only one way to find out . . .

• The wolf growled as if it were scared, too.

_____ took a deep breath and slowly
[Your Name Here]

held out the skeleton bone . . .

• _____ slid on the pumpkin helmet and
[Your Name Here]

turned to stare the Enderman right in the eyes . . .

• **Write the rest of your story here:**

_____

_____

_____

_____

_____

_____

_____

Read the words out loud. How do they make you feel?

Think of a title and turn the page.

ANOTHER COURAGEOUS COVER

Draw the book cover for your brave story below.

Add the title and the author's name—yours!

TURN MISTAKES INTO MASTERPIECES

Be brave enough to make mistakes. With every mistake, you learn something. You learn that the Overworld doesn't end. And you discover that good things can come from mistakes. Need proof?

Draw a scribble in the space below.

Now use crayons or colored pencils to turn that scribble into something beautiful: a sunset, a leafy tree, or the curly fur of a cute new critter. Turn your mistake into a masterpiece!

FIGHT BIG FEARS STEP BY STEP

Some worries are bigger than others. Let's say you're scared of wolves in Minecraft. How can you feel stronger?

Face your fear one step at a time.

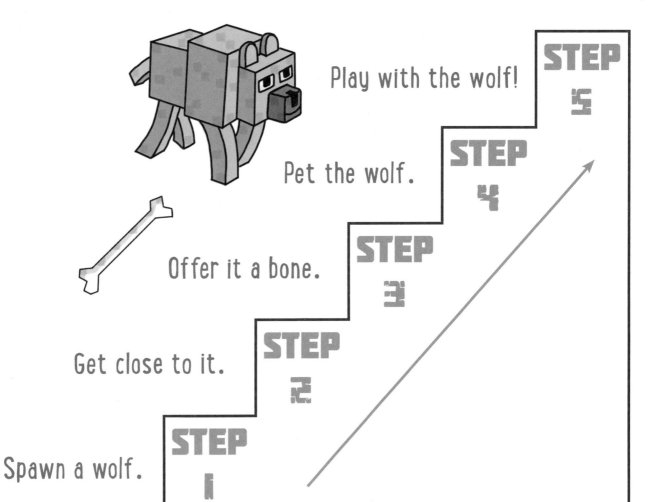

Play with the wolf!

Pet the wolf.

Offer it a bone.

Get close to it.

Spawn a wolf.

STEP 5

STEP 4

STEP 3

STEP 2

STEP 1

YOUR TURN!

Think of a big fear you have, and some smaller steps you can take to face that fear. Can't think of any steps? Ask a grown-up to help you.

Write the steps on the staircase below. *Hint:* Step 1 should be the easiest thing and Step 5 should be the hardest.

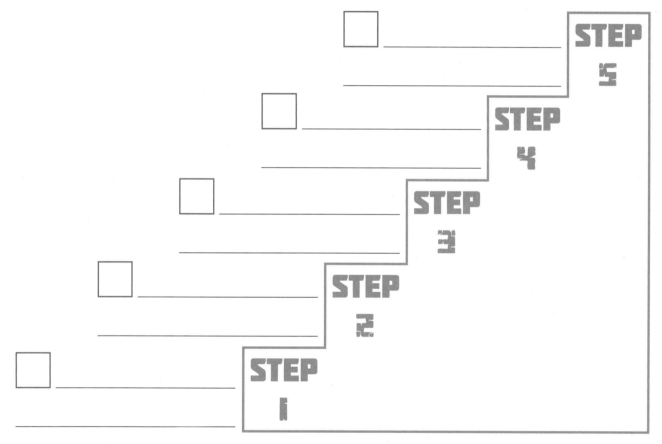

Imagine doing each step in your mind, and then start actually doing them. When you can do the first step without feeling scared, check it off and move to the second step. Take your time. Eventually, you'll make it all the way up!

TRY SOMETHING NEW

Being brave means sometimes saying YES to new things. Which of these could you say yes to?

Check at least three:

- ☐ Meeting a friend
- ☐ Eating a new food
- ☐ Starting a new hobby
- ☐ Watching a new show
- ☐ Wearing a new hairdo or hat
- ☐ Inventing a recipe
- ☐ Learning a word in a new language
- ☐ Going to a new restaurant
- ☐ Trying a new sport

BEE BRAVE

Picture a honeycomb. You have to brave the bees in order to get the honey, right? Sometimes we have to face our fears so that we can have or do something we *really* want.

Can you brave the bees and reach the sweet finish of this maze?

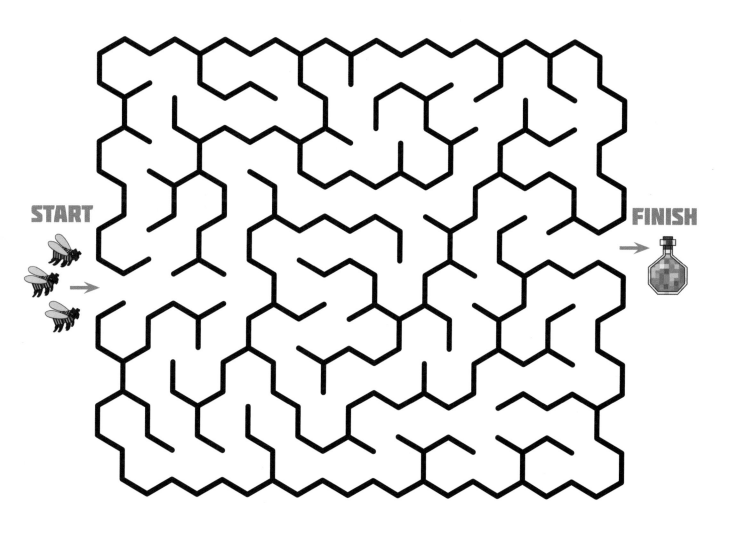

START

FINISH

PROTECT YOURSELF AND OTHERS

Being brave means sometimes saying NO to things that will hurt you or someone else.

Which of these would you be brave enough to say no to?

1. Would you let your friends bully someone?   **YES   NO**

2. Would you let someone copy your homework?   **YES   NO**

3. Would you tell a friend's secret to someone who asked?   **YES   NO**

4. Would you share an embarrassing photo of someone?   **YES   NO**

5. Would you break your parents' rules if a friend asked you to?   **YES   NO**

It doesn't matter how you say it—just say no. See how very brave you are!

SLOWLY BUT SURELY

When you're facing your fears, it's okay to move slowly. Just keep going in the right direction, step by step.

Connect the dots below to "spawn" another critter that moves slowly but surely forward.

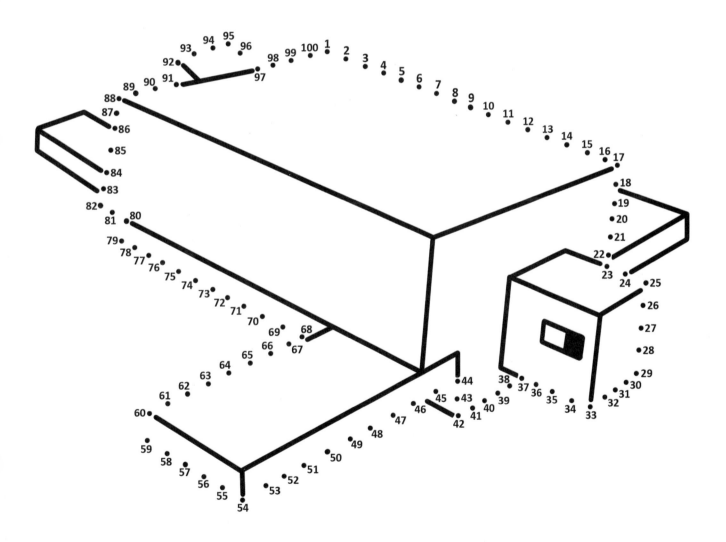

YOU GROW STRONGER

Every time you face your fears, you grow braver and stronger.

"Grow" the picture below by copying it, using the grid lines as a guide. Then add a brave expression and a smile.

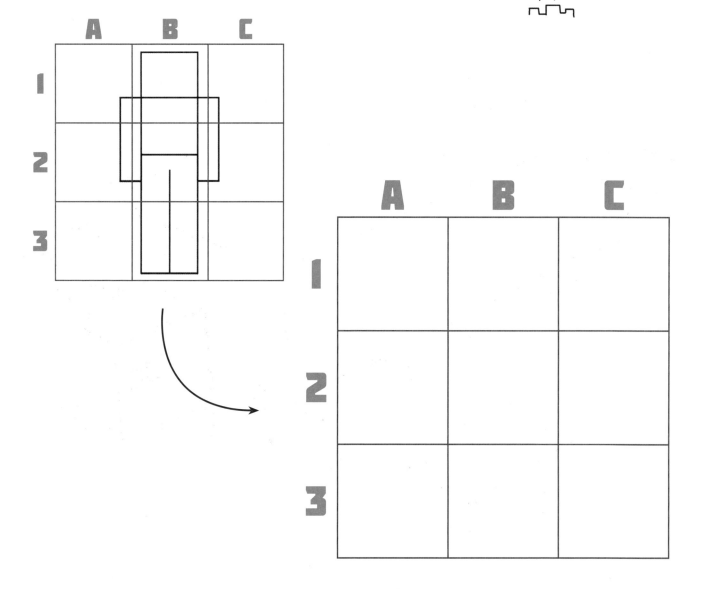

YOUR FEAR GROWS WEAKER

Every time you face your fears, *they* grow weaker.

"Shrink" the picture below by copying it into the smaller grid.

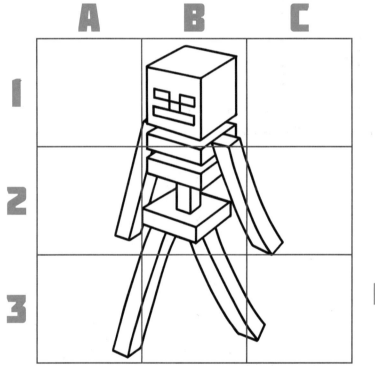

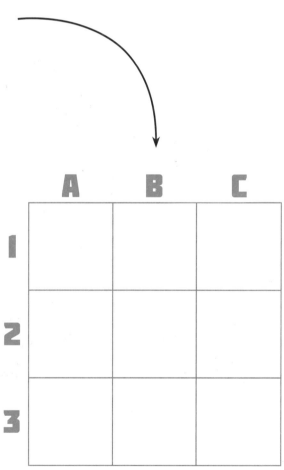

A POTION OF WEAKNESS

Doing something that scares you is like splashing your fear with a potion of Weakness.

Write some things you're scared of in the bottle below.

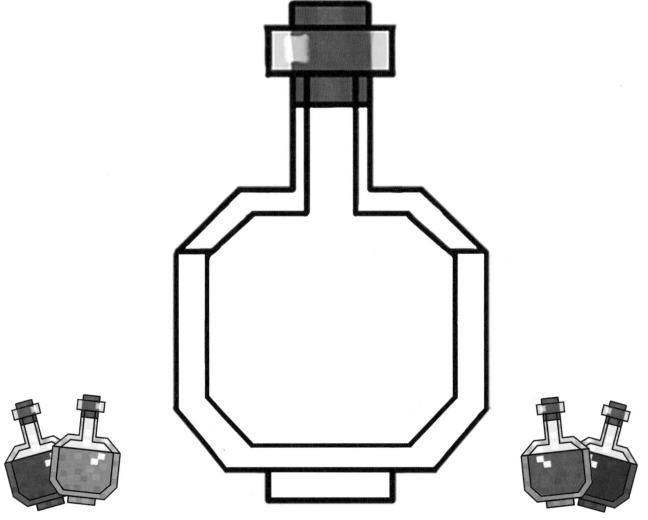

Now color over them with a crayon or colored pencil.
That's your "potion" weakening your fears when you face them head-on. Eventually, they'll be gone. *Poof!*

BE YOUR OWN BEST FRIEND

When you need a boost of courage, give yourself a pep talk—just like you would a friend.

Fill in the blanks below.

Hey, _____ ,
[Your Name Here]

I know you're feeling _____. That's okay—lots of kids feel

that way! But you'll get through this. You're a lot stronger than

you think you are. Here are some things I love most about you:

_____

_____.

You've got this. And I'm really proud of you!

_____
[Your Name Here]

TAKE INVENTORY

After reading this book, you have lots of tools to use the *next* time you're feeling scared.

For each tip you've tried, draw the picture next to it in your "inventory" below. Can you fill it up?

1. Shine the light on fear by talking about it with a friend.

2. Move your body. Get up and groove!

3. Take a pufferfish breath.

4. Practice a brave pose.

5. "Pop" scary thoughts like potion bubbles.

6. Catch and release worries like fish in the sea.

7. Use an imaginary portal to visit your peaceful place.

8. Stay calm by choosing healthy snacks.

9. Create a worry-free bedtime routine.

My inventory:

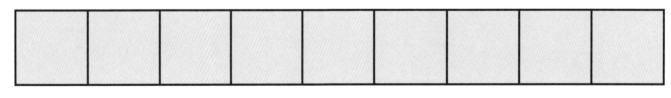

REMEMBER THIS

The next time you're feeling scared, what can you tell yourself?

Unscramble the words below to find out.

You're R-E-A-V-R-B _____

than you think you are.

You W-O-N-K _____ what to do.

You've T-G-O _____ this!

ANSWER KEY

Page 6

BEING BRAVE MEANS DOING OR FACING SOMETHING EVEN IF IT SCARES YOU.

Page 9

1. Because fear is like a **THIEF**. It can rob you of your confidence.

2. Because fear can keep you from **DOING** what you love and having **FUN**.

3. Because fear can **TRIP** you up like a tripwire and **STOP** you in your tracks.

4. Because the best way to make a fear grow **WEAKER** is to face it head-on.

Page 12

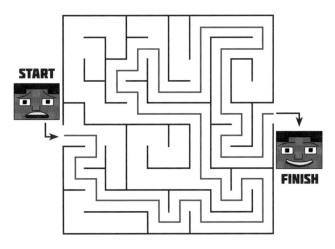

Page 14

1. Creepers avoid cats.
2. Zombies avoid sunlight.
3. Endermen avoid water.
4. Skeletons avoid wolves.

Page 21

A CHICKEN? HEY, THANKS FOR THE COMPLIMENT!

Page 26

1. **b**; 2. **d**; 3. **a**; 4. **c**

Page 29

1. You're **STRONGER** than you think you are.

2. If you **THINK** you can, you will.

3. **MISTAKES** are just proof that you're trying.

Page 32

Page 36

HEY KID WANT TO HAVE A STARING CONTEST?

Page 38

Page 42

```
P N H P F C O S J B R E H Z E
U R Z T Y E H C P N Y E C L U
U Y F G B Q O P N R O C A V P
N F I L Z B F N E J G A I Y X
D U Y K O Y A H X H U R Q P F
U J X Q B L D N V V R R L M C
R P A U P I C X A J T O O Y S
B D A T H O N Q B N R T B B G
P P A Z P R P L M R A S C Y E
A P P L E S I C Z D C S E R E
U P V A A E G L O N O N L L Z
H N R A I S I N S R N F E X I
V U C H E E S E V U N M R L L
W T P K M B N M V H P T Y E D
S S H D L B E R R I E S F H M
```

Page 53

START

FINISH

Page 55

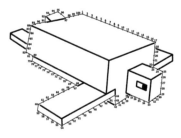

Page 61

You're **BRAVER** than you think you are. You **KNOW** what to do. You've **GOT** this!